T0265488

Sweet Spreads

Sweet Spreads

Delectable Dessert Boards for Every Occasion

Amber Olson

creator of SimplyMadeRecipes.com

Skyhorse Publishing

Skyhorse Publishing books may be purchased in bulk at special discounts for sales promotion, corporate gifts, fund-raising, or educational purposes. Special editions can also be created to specifications. For details, contact the Special Sales Department, Skyhorse Publishing, 307 West 36th Street, 11th Floor, New York, NY 10018 or info@skyhorsepublishing.com.

Skyhorse® and Skyhorse Publishing® are registered trademarks of Skyhorse Publishing, Inc.®, a Delaware corporation.

Visit our website at www.skyhorsepublishing.com.

10 9 8 7 6 5 4 3 2 1

Library of Congress Cataloging-in-Publication Data is available on file.

Cover design by Daniel Brount and David Ter-Avanesyan
Cover photo by Amber Olson

Print ISBN: 978-1-5107-6996-0
Ebook ISBN: 978-1-5107-6998-4

Printed in China

For my late grandmother, who nurtured my love for food through her endless encouragement and guidance.

Table of Contents

Introduction

"Cooking is one of the great gifts you can give to those you love."
—Ina Garten

I started cooking when I was very young. Some of my fondest childhood memories are of being in the kitchen at my grandmother's house. We would pick fresh blackberries out on the property and bring them inside to make homemade pies. I would have to stand on a chair to be able to reach the kitchen counter as my grandmother patiently taught me how to create pie crust from scratch and add the perfect amount of sugar to the berries for the most delicious pie filling. This is the kitchen where my love of food began.

Life blessed me with a large family consisting of uncles, aunts, and a whole lot of cousins. Family gatherings, especially holidays, have always been a little bit insane. That very kitchen where my love for food began also became the center of every family event. Kitchen counters lined with beautiful desserts, amazing charcuterie spreads, and comfort foods galore turned food into a vessel to share conversation, laughter, and a lot of special moments in my life. These moments are what inspired me to write this book.

I intend for you to use these recipes as inspiration to help create your own cherished memories with food as the centerpiece. Holidays, birthdays, date nights with your significant other, movie nights with the family, neighborhood barbecues, lunch with your best friends, or any occasion can be special. Something as simple as a beautiful dessert board can be the perfect starting point.

Chapter 1

How to Create the Perfect Dessert Board

Let us get into what a dessert board is and how to achieve building your own. First, you need an occasion. This occasion could be a big event in your life, like hosting a baby shower for your closest friend or a holiday with the entire family. This occasion could also be something seemingly less spectacular like that weekly scheduled date night with your significant other or a friend popping by for coffee on the weekend. Whatever the occasion may be, there is a dessert board to generate a spark of wow and engagement.

So, what is a dessert board exactly?

Think of a dessert board much like a charcuterie board where you have a lot of little snackable items presented in a really appealing way on a single board or tray. However, unlike a classic charcuterie board, a dessert board does not have a straightforward list of what must be added or combined. This allows for you to be as creative as you wish. The single must-have for a dessert board is something sweet. Candy, chocolates, cakes, cookies, pastries, donuts, marshmallows, caramels, pies, and fresh fruits are all good ideas for that something sweet, but the options are endless. With that being said, I have put together some step-by-step instructions to help you pull together a jaw-dropping dessert board for anytime followed by fifty sweet spreads I have created myself for your own inspiration.

Pick a Theme

Once you know what occasion you are creating a dessert board for, you can pick a theme for your board. There are obvious themes to fit the occasion like Valentine's Day where you can go overboard on heart-shaped goodies. There are also some not so obvious themes such as hosting a night at your house with a few close friends. In this case, think about something you all enjoy. If you all love wine, then a theme of chocolate and cheese would be perfect.

Grab Ingredients

Once you have a theme for the occasion you choose, it is time to grab all the ingredients that will be put onto your dessert board. Some boards will come together flawlessly with a visit to your regular grocery store. Fruit, nuts, and chocolates, for example. Boom. Done. Easy. Some boards will take more effort by sourcing the perfect sprinkles or finding a bakery to make some really creative sugar cookies. An amazing part of the world we live in is that there are all sorts of avenues to find these special items. A quick Google search will get you in contact with a local bakery or candy store that can assist you. Of course, online ordering for basically anything you could possibly imagine makes it possible to create that extravagant dessert board you have pictured in your head.

Where to Begin

Have a great idea but not sure where to begin? Trust me, I know this feeling. My best is advice is to start by finding one special item that will inspire you. Personally, I get really inspired by finding the perfect sprinkles or cutest decorative sugar cookies. Once you have those perfect sprinkles, for example, you have a direction. Start finding items in the same color palette as those sprinkles and the board will basically build itself.

Here are some of my favorite ingredients to shop for:

- Sprinkles
- Cupcake liners
- Chocolates
- Nuts
- Fresh fruits
- Dried fruits
- Pretzels
- Cheeses
- Cookies
- Decorative sugar cookies
- Crackers
- Truffles
- Trail mix
- Donuts
- Prepackaged treats like miniature cakes
- Scones
- Macarons
- Taffy
- Biscotti
- Edible flowers

Pick a Board

You have an occasion. You have a theme. You bought the ingredients. Now it is time to pick a board to present all these items on. Some of my favorite things to build a dessert board on are pizza boards, large cutting boards, serving trays, and even baking sheets. When building a dessert board that will be traveling with you somewhere, I recommend using a serving tray with sides to easily transport or taking the ingredients separately to assemble at the event so that everything turns out perfectly.

Here are my most-used dessert boards:

- 17" round serving tray
- 13" round pizza board
- 10" × 20" cutting board
- 11" × 14" serving tray
- 13" × 17" serving tray
- 11" × 17" baking sheet
- 12" × 18" serving tray
- 14" round serving tray
- 6" × 7" cutting board
- 9" × 13" serving tray
- 4" × 4" boards
- 8" × 14" rectangular serving tray

Assembly

Time for the fun part: assembling the board to prepare for serving. Some items on the board may be homemade and need some time to prep or rest, so think about the time needed in advance so that your board will be complete when it is needed. Next, get ramekins or small bowls out to hold any accompaniments. Prepare to have extras on the side to refill these small items as the gathering goes on. This also goes for items like mini-cupcakes. Maybe only six cupcakes will fit on the board for presentation, so have some set to the side to refill your board as needed. If you want to carry on enjoying yourself without having to worry about refilling the board, these accompaniments can be presented off the board as well. Think about a cupcake stand next to the board or larger bowls or plates.

Here are some items I use often:

- Ramekins
- Small bowls
- Plates on the side
- Bowls on the side
- Miniature .5-quart Dutch oven for warm dips
- Serving utensils

Take It Step-by-Step

Place ramekins or small bowls on your board for accompaniments. Spread them out in different sections. Next, put larger items on the board to fill in any open areas. At this step, you will want to pay attention to color and texture. If decorative cupcakes are going in one section, the opposite section should hold something just as decorative or colorful to balance it out and bring the focus to all items on the board as opposed to just one colorful area. Then, fill in the gaps of the board with smaller items like fresh fruit. Fresh fruit is probably my favorite way to fill in a board. You add color, freshness, texture, and beauty with something as simple as a handful of raspberries. Finally, add a special touch. Edible flowers, a vibrant garnish, or some sprinkles tossed on top can go a long way for a board's overall appearance.

Chapter 2

Chocolate Lovers

Chocolate Hummus Dessert Board

Serve on a 17" round serving tray

A healthier option for a chocolate fix, this board can be made for any occasion at any time throughout the year. A beautiful and creamy hummus is paired with fresh fruits and snackable bites of cheese, pretzels, and nuts. I love this indulgent board because everything can be eaten guilt-free.

INGREDIENTS

Chocolate Hummus (recipe on page 125)

8 ounces Monterey Jack cheese, cubed

½ cup pistachios

½ cup salted cashews

½ cup banana chips

1 bundle grapes

1 cup pretzel twists

3 mandarin oranges

1 cup blueberries

1 cup strawberries

3 kiwis

1 cup grape tomatoes

INSTRUCTIONS

1. Add the Chocolate Hummus to a small ramekin or bowl on your serving tray.

2. Place the remaining ingredients around the hummus. Be aware of color with this board. The cheese, nuts, and banana chips have a similar color palette and should be placed in different sections of the board.

Chocolate Tasting Dessert Board

Serve on a 13" round pizza board

The mood is chocolate. Dark chocolate, salty chocolate, milk chocolate, crunchy chocolate, creamy chocolate, and fruity chocolate. Raspberries add some freshness and color. Gorgeous enough to serve for a date night or to share a bottle of red wine with friends on the weekend.

INGREDIENTS

8 Chocolate-Covered Strawberries (recipe on page 126)

1 cup chocolate-covered almonds

7 dark chocolate squares

1 cup milk chocolate–dipped pretzels

7 ounces dark chocolate sea salt caramels

2 milk chocolate bars

3 chocolate truffles

1 cup fresh raspberries

INSTRUCTIONS

1. Place Chocolate-Covered Strawberries neatly on a section of your board.

2. Add chocolate-covered almonds to a small ramekin or bowl and place slightly off-center on your board.

3. Line dark chocolate squares down the center of the board.

4. Place milk chocolate–dipped pretzels on another section of your board.

5. Place dark chocolate sea salt caramels on another section of your board.

6. Break up the milk chocolate bars and add to board in a couple different spots.

7. In an open area, add chocolate truffles.

8. Fill in any open spots with some fresh raspberries for a pop of color and freshness.

Chocolate, Nut, and Fruit Dessert Board

Serve on a 10" × 20" cutting board

Sweet and salty come together in this jaw-dropping board without a lot of effort. A tantalizing chocolate cheesecake dip pairs with fresh fruits and an assortment of nuts. This board will definitely have everyone coming back for more.

INGREDIENTS

Chocolate Cheesecake Dip
   (recipe on page 129)

9 dark chocolate squares

1 cup cherries

1 cup raspberries

1 cup strawberries

15 dark chocolate sea salt
   caramels

½ cup salted cashews

½ cup salted almonds

½ cup pistachios

Fresh flowers, to garnish

Cookies or crackers, for serving

INSTRUCTIONS

1. Place Chocolate Cheesecake Dip into a small ramekin or bowl on your board.

2. Fan the dark chocolate squares around the chocolate cheesecake dip.

3. Place fruit onto your board in groupings.

4. Place a grouping of dark chocolate sea salt caramels on board.

5. Fill in empty spots of board with the cashews, almonds, and pistachios.

6. Garnish with some fresh flowers.

7. Cookies or crackers are also nice to serve on the side with this board to enjoy the Chocolate Cheesecake Dip.

S'mores Dessert Board

Serve on a 17" round serving tray

Bring the flavor of s'mores into your home any time of year! This dessert board is especially great with kids for the easy-to-grab S'mores Snack Mix and the fun of the gooey marshmallow and chocolate S'mores Dip. A real treat for the whole family.

INGREDIENTS

S'mores Snack Mix (recipe on page 131)

S'mores Dip (recipe on page 132)

4 graham crackers

9 chewy chocolate chip cookies

8 chocolate stroopwafels (waffle cookies)

14 coconut cookies

1 cup chocolate-dipped peanuts

1 cup fresh strawberries

INSTRUCTIONS

1. Add the S'mores Snack Mix to a bowl.

2. Add the S'mores Dip to a .5 quart Dutch oven. Serve hot for that delicious melty chocolate and gooey marshmallow.

3. Place both the S'mores Snack Mix and S'mores Dip onto your board. Note that the S'mores Dip is hot and should sit on a heat resistant trivet so that it does not do damage to your board.

4. Break the graham crackers into small dippable rectangles and fan out from the S'mores Dip.

5. Fan out the chocolate chip cookies away from the S'mores Dip.

6. Add the chocolate stroopwafels to a large open space on your board followed by the coconut cookies in a nice row.

7. Fill in any open areas with chocolate-dipped peanuts and fresh strawberries.

Date Night Dessert Board

Serve on a 6" × 7" cutting board

Do date night different with this chocolatey encounter prepared for two. Cozy up with this mini board and a glass of wine on the couch to finish off a dinner date at home. A warm fire coming from the fireplace and a soft blanket (or wine of choice) to pair will surely be the spark of a memorable night with your partner.

INGREDIENTS

4 dark chocolate sea salt caramels

4 chocolate truffles

4 dark chocolate squares

2 chocolate macarons

1 handful pistachios

4 dried mission figs

½ cup fresh raspberries

INSTRUCTIONS

1. Arrange the chocolate items on your board, spreading them in groupings.

2. Fill in any empty spots with pistachios, figs, and raspberries.

Peanut Butter and Chocolate Dessert Board

Serve on a 17" round serving tray

A full board dedicated to one of the most genius food combinations on the planet: peanut butter and chocolate. Every bite taken from this board bursts with the peanut butter and chocolate combo you crave.

INGREDIENTS

Peanut Butter Dip (recipe on page 139), make right before serving

1 (10-ounce) package fudge chocolate crème cookies

1 pound peanut butter OREO cookies

Nutter Butter Balls (recipe on page 155), keep refrigerated until ready to serve

5 ounces peanut butter and chocolate muddy buddies

12 ounces peanut butter cups

1 cup peanut butter and chocolate trail mix

INSTRUCTIONS

1. Add the Peanut Butter Dip to a small ramekin or bowl and place on tray.

2. Arrange the fudge chocolate crème cookies around the peanut butter dip.

3. Line the peanut butter OREO cookies around the tray.

4. Line the Nutter Butter Balls in front of the peanut butter OREO cookies.

5. Fill in the large empty spaces with the peanut butter and chocolate muddy buddies and peanut butter cups.

6. Fill in any extra space on tray with the peanut butter and chocolate trail mix.

Mint Chocolate Dessert Board

Serve on an 11" × 14" serving tray

The rich chocolate combined with cooling mint flavors in this recipe will have everyone coming back for more. Perfect for a holiday party or for any occasion, this board is easy to create, easy to serve, and loaded with flavor.

INGREDIENTS

Mint Chocolate Dip (recipe on page 140)

16 mint flavor crème OREO cookies

1 (3-ounce) package KIT KAT® dark chocolate candy bars

1 (1½-ounce) package KIT KAT® DUOS mint + dark chocolate candy bars

1 (11-ounce) box mint striped fudge cookies

1 cup dark chocolate mint swirl chocolates, unwrapped

1 handful crème de menthe mints, unwrapped

8 ounces chocolate-dipped pretzels

INSTRUCTIONS

1. Add the Mint Chocolate Dip to a small ramekin or bowl and place off-center on your board.

2. Create a half circle around the Mint Chocolate Dip with the mint flavor crème OREO cookies.

3. Break apart and line up all the KIT KAT® candy bars between the mint striped fudge cookies and the OREO cookies.

4. Place the dark chocolate mint swirl chocolates in a large open area on the board.

5. Place the crème de menthe mints in open space on the board.

6. Fill in any remaining open space with chocolate-dipped pretzels.

Mini Chocolate Dessert Boards

Serve on 4" × 4" boards

Individualized boards are all the rage right now. They are so tiny but pack in a huge amount of character for entertaining. Chocolate truffles and custard-filled chocolate-covered éclairs pair just right with fresh blackberries, pecans, and crunchy peanut brittle. Perfect for a dinner party with friends or family! Once you make these, mini boards may just become your go-to dessert.

INGREDIENTS

1 mini chocolate-covered éclair dusted with powdered sugar

5 pecan halves

1 piece peanut brittle

1 Belgian cocoa-dusted chocolate truffle

3 fresh blackberries

INSTRUCTIONS

1. Place the mini chocolate-covered éclair on one corner of board.

2. Add pecan halves in center of board.

3. Place peanut brittle in a corner of board.

4. Place chocolate truffle in another corner.

5. Fill any empty space with blackberries.

6. Repeat steps above for all other mini boards.

Cheese and Chocolate Dessert Board

Serve on a 17" round serving tray

A board filled with cheese, chocolate, crackers, nuts, and fresh fruit will be a showstopper for your next gathering. The perfect board to put out before dinner for guests to snack on. Bonus if you offer a few different wines to pair! What is there not to love about this board? There is something for everyone and all ingredients are easily found at your local grocery so you can add a special touch to a spur-of-the-moment party.

INGREDIENTS

7 ounces aged cheddar cheese, cubed

5.5 ounces blue cheese

5.3 ounces double Gloucester cheese, sliced

½ cup pistachios

6.5 ounces sea salt scalloped crackers

4 ounces sea salt and olive oil breadstick crackers

3 ounces everything bagel flatbread crackers

1 cup dark chocolate almonds

3 ounces hazelnut cookies with chocolate base

2 (1.55-ounce) milk chocolate bars

1 (4.25-ounce) dark chocolate bar

1 cup fresh strawberries

½ cup fresh raspberries

½ cup salted almonds

INSTRUCTIONS

1. Arrange the three types of cheeses in different areas on your board.

2. Add pistachios to a small ramekin or bowl and place off-center on your board.

3. Spread the three types of crackers in groupings around your board.

4. Fill in large spaces with dark chocolate almonds, hazelnut cookies, and chocolate bars, breaking up the chocolate bars as needed to fit.

5. Add fresh fruit to board.

6. Place the salted almonds in any open space left to fill.

Sweet and Salty Dessert Board

Serve on a 13" round pizza board

Sweet and salty bites create a balanced board that you can serve during any occasion for both adults and children to enjoy. I love the simplicity of this board. It isn't terribly fancy but still looks beautiful and has something for everyone.

INGREDIENTS

Cranberry and Salted Peanut Chocolate Bark (recipe on page 150), cut into squares

½ cup cranberry medley trail mix

9 ounces dark chocolate sea salt caramels

1 handful pretzels filled with peanut butter

1+ cup popcorn, freshly popped

4 ounces dark chocolate pecan bark

6 fresh strawberries

½ cup fresh raspberries

INSTRUCTIONS

1. Place the chocolate bark around the corner of a quarter of the board.

2. Pour cranberry medley trail mix into a small ramekin or bowl and place it near the chocolate bark.

3. On the opposite side of board, stack the dark chocolate sea salt caramels next to the pretzels filled with peanut butter.

4. Fill the center of your board with popcorn.

5. Fill in any remaining open areas of your board with a grouping of dark chocolate pecan bark, strawberries, and raspberries.

Chocolate Fondue Dessert Board

Serve on an 11" × 14" serving tray

A rich and creamy chocolate fondue is always a fun way to serve a shareable dessert with minimal effort. Kids and adults alike will love picking out their favorite sweet treats and dunking them in delicious chocolate. This board is amazing if you want a lot of variation to make your own. The chocolate fondue can be paired with anything that can be dipped in chocolate (and I do mean *anything*)!

INGREDIENTS

Chocolate Fondue Dip (recipe on page 128), make right before serving

1 (10-ounce) butter pound cake, cubed

Rice Krispies Treats™ (recipe on page 127), cut into squares

1+ cup glazed donut holes

1+ cup marshmallows

10 ounces fresh strawberries

INSTRUCTIONS

1. Add the chocolate fondue dip to a small ramekin or bowl in the center of your tray.

2. Place the butter pound cake in a corner of your tray.

3. Place the Rise Krispies Treats™ opposite the butter pound cake since they are relatively similar in color.

4. Fill in a section with glazed donut holes and another section with marshmallows.

5. Cover any remaining area of the tray with strawberries for a pop of fresh color.

6. Serve with skewers on the side for easy dipping.

Chapter 3

Boards for Any Occasion

Movie Night Dessert Board

Serve on a 13" round pizza board

Everyone's snack favorites put on one shareable board will call for more epic movie nights at home. This board is a winner for family move nights, date night, or fun slumber parties! Easily swap in your preferred candies, crackers, cheeses, and fruits so you have a household of enthusiastic faces ready for the movies.

INGREDIENTS

1 (3-ounce) bag buttered popcorn, popped

½ cup M&M's®

½ cup gummy bears

1 sleeve crackers

4 slices cheddar cheese, quartered

4 slices Swiss cheese, quartered

1 handful licorice

1 handful grapes

½ cup strawberries, halved lengthwise

½ cup animal crackers

1 cup caramel corn

INSTRUCTIONS

1. Place popcorn in a bowl on the board.

2. Add M&M's® and gummy bears to small ramekins or bowls on and/or around the board.

3. Fan out the crackers and cheese around the candy bowls.

4. Fill in a large open space with licorice and another with grapes.

5. Fill in any extra spots with strawberries, animal crackers, and caramel corn.

Afternoon Tea Dessert Board

Serve on an 8" × 14" rectangular serving tray

Take time to unwind and relax with a board that will inspire you to slow down for a moment. Afternoon tea pairs nicely with a few sweet treats and great conversation with some of your closest friends. Instead of going out for a boozy brunch, host a quaint gathering at your house and just sit back and enjoy the company.

INGREDIENTS

12 lemon dunkers

8 honey stroopwafels

6 mini orange scones

10 apricot honey phyllo crisps

12 butter cookies coated with milk chocolate

6 lemon macarons

6 honey vanilla chamomile tea bags

5 honey stirrers

INSTRUCTIONS

1. Place the lemon dunkers on a plate to the side of your tray.

2. Arrange stroopwafels in the center of your tray.

3. Place remaining ingredients in tidy rows on either side of stroopwafels.

Sweet Waffle Brunch Board

Serve on a 10" × 20" cutting board

A sweet spread isn't just dessert. Make brunch the sweetest part of the day with homemade waffles, cinnamon rolls, and fresh fruits. This board is ideal for serving when you have guests stay the night. Simply place it on the center of the kitchen table or island as everyone is waking up in the morning.

INGREDIENTS

Waffles (recipe on page 130)

1 cup maple syrup

1 cup caramel sauce

16 mini cinnamon rolls

1 pound bacon

1 orange, sliced

1 grapefruit, sliced

1 cup fresh berries (I used strawberries, blueberries, and blackberries)

INSTRUCTIONS

1. Lay waffles out all the way down your board.

2. Add maple syrup to a syrup dispenser and place on your board.

3. Warm up caramel sauce in microwave for 30 seconds to 1 minute and add to a small ramekin or bowl on board.

4. Place mini cinnamon rolls on board in groupings to take up large open areas.

5. Add bacon to board.

6. Fill in any remaining open areas with the orange, grapefruit, and fresh berries.

7. Serve with a side of juice if desired.

Donut Board

Serve on a 13" round cutting board

Why serve donuts in a box when a gorgeous board can be made to showcase these sweet goodies? This may be the single easiest board to toss together. All you need are your favorite donuts, some bacon, a little green garnish, and fresh berries for a pop of color—proving that the simplest food presentation can go a long way!

INGREDIENTS

6 fresh rosemary sprigs

10 donuts, assorted flavors

6 slices crispy bacon

9+ donut holes

1 handful fresh raspberries

INSTRUCTIONS

1. Spread out the rosemary in different areas of your board.

2. Spread out the donuts on your board.

3. Spread out the crispy bacon on your board.

4. Fill in large gaps with the donut holes.

5. Fill in any remaining space with fresh raspberries.

Summer Picnic Dessert Board

Serve on a 17" round serving tray

The real star of this dessert board is a hand pie made with love and presented beautifully among fresh fruits and a whipped cream topping. This board is easy to take with you to a family outing at the park or a friend's house on a hot day.

INGREDIENTS

2 cups Whipped Cream (recipe on page 154)

18 blueberry, raspberry, and strawberry Jam and Cream Cheese Hand Pies (recipe on page 115)

2 cups blueberries

2 cups strawberries

2 cups raspberries

INSTRUCTIONS

1. Add Whipped Cream to a small ramekin or bowl and place in the center of your tray.

2. Arrange Jam and Cream Cheese Hand Pies around your tray in groupings of flavors.

3. Place fresh fruits into any empty spaces.

Campfire Cones Dessert Board

Serve on a 9" × 13" serving tray

Classic s'mores are so last summer with these fun campfire cone creations! Sugar cones are filled with gooey marshmallows, melty chocolate, fruit, or candies for a new favorite dessert to make while sitting by the fire on a chilly night. This board is really exciting to serve because everyone gets to create something with the ingredients. It is so much more than a dessert board.

INGREDIENTS

10 sugar cones

1 cup Golden Grahams™ cereal

1 cup mini marshmallows

½ cup fresh strawberries, diced

1 banana, sliced

2 chocolate bars, broken into bite size chunks

½ cup salted peanuts

½ cup M&M's®

INSTRUCTIONS

1. Arrange cones diagonally across your tray.

2. Add the Golden Grahams™ cereal and marshmallows in opposite groupings on your tray.

3. Add the fresh strawberries and bananas into separate groupings on your tray.

4. Fill any empty spots with remaining ingredients.

To make the s'mores campfire cones:

1. Fill each cone with marshmallows and other desired toppings.
2. Wrap filled cone in aluminum foil.
3. Using tongs, place wrapped cone into campfire for 5 minutes.
4. Unwrap and enjoy!

Autumn Dessert Board

Serve on a 13" × 17" serving tray

A delicious pumpkin dip is the centerpiece of this beautiful autumn-inspired dessert board. You will find lots of cookies and crackers to dip into this creamy pumpkin dip and little snackable bites like caramels, nuts, and fruits throughout. This board will be impressive for any fall event, even Thanksgiving!

INGREDIENTS

Pumpkin Cheesecake Dip (recipe on page 133), keep refrigerated until ready to serve

Decorative pumpkins, to garnish

2 dozen vanilla wafer cookies

14 maple leaf cream cookies

6 graham crackers

1 handful caramels

16 apple cinnamon phyllo crisps

2 apples, sliced

1 pear, sliced

¼ cup pumpkin seeds

½ cup pecans

1 handful Belgian chocolate pumpkin candies

INSTRUCTIONS

1. Add Pumpkin Cheesecake Dip to a small ramekin or bowl on your tray.

2. Spread out decorative pumpkins (if using) around your tray.

3. Arrange vanilla wafer cookies, maple leaf cream cookies, and graham crackers around dip.

4. Place caramels in a corner of your tray.

5. Place cinnamon phyllo crisps in 2 rows on the opposite corner of your tray.

6. Add apples and pear to your tray.

7. Fill any empty spots with pumpkin seeds and pecans.

8. Add the finishing touch with some tiny Belgian chocolate pumpkin candies.

Bundt Cakes Dessert Board

Serve on a 13" round pizza board

Your friends will enjoy these mini Bundt cakes made special for them with fresh fruits galore to pair. This board adds so much vibrant color to a dessert table with the generous number of various berries and peach slices.

INGREDIENTS

8 Mini Bundt Cakes (recipe on page 134)

Icing (recipe on page 135)

1 peach, sliced

1 cup strawberries, halved

1 cup raspberries

1 cup blackberries

INSTRUCTIONS

1. Place the Mini Bundt Cakes on your board.

2. Add icing to a small ramekin or bowl on your board. Icing is best served freshly made.

3. Add the fresh fruit around your board, making sure to cover any empty spots and spread out the different fruit colors for visual appeal.

4. Have friends grab a mini Bundt cake, drizzle with icing, and eat with plenty of fresh fruits of their choosing.

Caramel Apple Dessert Board

Serve on a 10" × 20" cutting board

Caramel sauce covered in goodies is guaranteed to please any caramel lover. Caramel apples are typically a fall-inspired dessert but this board can offer that favorite fall flavor anytime, anywhere!

INGREDIENTS

1 cup mini marshmallows

1 cup rainbow sprinkles

1 cup chopped pecans

1 cup mini M&M's®

Caramel Apple Dip (recipe on page 136)

14 ounces gingersnap cookies

16 ounces caramels

3 apples, sliced

1 (10-ounce) jar caramel sauce

INSTRUCTIONS

1. Add mini marshmallows, rainbow sprinkles, chopped pecans, mini M&M's®, and Caramel Apple Dip to small ramekins or bowls and spread out on your board.

2. Create a circle with gingersnap cookies around the chopped pecans and a half circle around the marshmallows.

3. Fill in a large space with the caramels.

4. Fill in any gaps on board with apples.

5. Before serving, warm up the jar of caramel sauce and place it on the side of your board. Friends can dip apples into the caramel and sprinkle their favorite toppings on top.

Rainbow Dessert Board

Serve on a 9" × 13" serving tray

Brighten up your day with all the colors of the rainbow on this candy-covered board that is dazzling to the eyes and to the taste buds. This board is all about the bright colors and having fun with candy. It's especially exciting to serve to kids to celebrate something special or just to say well done on a big accomplishment in their lives.

INGREDIENTS

7 ounces red licorice

5 yellow macarons

1 cup mini gumballs

6 large rainbow swirled lollipops

1 (8-ounce) package Ultimate Party Cake Bites

1 (7-ounce) package multicolored gummy candy streamers

2 cups multicolored Tutti Frutti Popcorn

INSTRUCTIONS

1. Place licorice in a corner of your tray.

2. Line up the yellow macarons next to the licorice.

3. Add mini gumballs to a small ramekin or bowl on the opposite side of your tray next to the rainbow swirled lollipops.

4. Line up the Ultimate Party Cake Bites in a large empty spot.

5. Fill in any other large empty spots by lining up the different colors of gummy candy streamers into rows.

6. Dump the Tutti Frutti Popcorn in the center of your tray to fill in remaining gaps.

Coffee-Inspired Dessert Board

Serve on an 11" × 14" serving tray

A simple, delicious tray of goodies to pair with a fresh, hot cup of coffee is always a great idea. The idea behind this board is to have something to toss together quickly when guests come over that is presented beautifully to make them feel at home. A simple cup of coffee and a bite of something sweet goes a long way to bring comfort.

INGREDIENTS

8 ounces honey stroopwafels

9 dark chocolate pizzelles

6 ounces dark chocolate Milano® cookies

6 pecan biscotti

16 chocolate hazelnut pirouettes

10 ounces dark chocolate espresso beans

INSTRUCTIONS

1. Line the honey stroopwafels on one end of your tray and the chocolate pizzelles on the other.

2. Place the dark chocolate Milano® cookies down one side of your tray and tuck in the pecan biscotti next to them.

3. Fill in the remaining open space with hazelnut pirouettes and dark chocolate espresso beans.

4. Serve with hot coffee and mugs on the side.

Ice Cream Dessert Board

Serve on a 13" round cutting board

Create amazing memories with this board by pairing a simple no-churn ice cream with everything from candy and chocolates to nuts and fresh fruits. It's sure to be fun for the whole family!

INGREDIENTS

½ cup maraschino cherries

½ cup rainbow sprinkles

½ cup chopped pecans

4–6 waffle cones

½ banana, sliced

1 cup marshmallows

1 cup M&M's®

1 cup sour gummy worms

1 handful blueberries

1 handful raspberries

No-Churn Vanilla Ice Cream
    (recipe on page 143), make
    6–12 hours before serving

INSTRUCTIONS

1. Add the maraschino cherries, rainbow sprinkles, and chopped pecans into small ramekins or bowls and spread out on your board.

2. Place waffle cones toward the edge of board with bananas next to them.

3. Fill in open areas with separate groupings of marshmallows, M&M's®, sour gummy worms, blueberries, and raspberries.

4. Serve ice cream on the side and top with any or all ingredients listed above.

Top off your ice cream with chocolate syrup, caramel sauce, and whipped cream!

Winter Wonderland Dessert Board

Serve on a 9" × 13" serving tray

Let it snow, let it snow, let it snow! Take a walk in a winter wonderland with treats of white and shades of blue. A great board to serve on a holiday like Christmas or New Year's or any other gathering where you'd wish for a little snow to magically appear.

INGREDIENTS

6 Mini Vanilla Cupcakes (recipe on page 118) with Vanilla Buttercream Frosting (recipe on page 119) and blue sprinkles

4.6 ounces blue raspberry gumballs

2 cups blue raspberry taffy

6 blue rock candy swizzle sticks

8 ounces yogurt-covered pretzels

7.4 ounces M&M's® white chocolate pretzel snowballs

3–6 mini snowman sugar cookies

INSTRUCTIONS

1. Add decorated cupcakes to tray in a nice line.

2. Add gumballs to a small ramekin or bowl and place on tray.

3. Place blue raspberry taffy on one side of your tray.

4. On opposite side of tray, add blue rock candy swizzle sticks in a nice pile.

5. Fill in a large open spot with yogurt-covered pretzels.

6. Drop the M&M's® into any remaining empty space on your tray.

7. Place sugar cookies on top of taffy to break up all the blue color or anywhere on or around your tray that needs a bit more decoration.

Back-to-School Dessert Board

Serve on an 8" × 14" rectangular serving tray

Back to school can be a stressful time of year for kids and parents alike. Create a little fun in the home with some goodies to celebrate back-to-school time and inspire a great school year!

INGREDIENTS

1 handful Smarties® Candy

6 school-inspired sugar cookies (apples and pencils are pictured here)

6 red macarons

6 mini boxes Grape & Strawberry NERDS

1 handful Big Chewy NERDS candy

2 × 2.6-ounce packages efrutti® Planet Gummi candies, unwrapped

INSTRUCTIONS

1. Place Smarties® Candy on one end of tray.

2. Place a neat row of sugar cookies on the other end.

3. Make a row of red macarons on the opposite edge of tray.

4. Make a row of mini boxes of NERDS next to the red macarons.

5. Fill in the empty space with a handful of Big Chewy NERDS.

6. Complete this tray with the planet gummi candies to fill any leftover space.

Put these board items into a small box to give as a teacher present.

Rose Dessert Board

Serve on a 13" round cutting board

There are some serious love vibes with this rose-inspired board of pink champagne cupcakes and crunchy chocolate rose bark. Serve this board on Valentine's Day or during a night in with the girls (while sharing a bottle of champagne)!

INGREDIENTS

Rose and Pistachio Chocolate Bark (recipe on page 148)

6 pink macarons

8 Champagne Cupcakes (recipe on page 120), with champagne frosting and dried rose petal garnish

Chocolate-Covered Strawberries (recipe on page 126), with chocolate drizzle

1 cup pistachios

1½ cups fresh raspberries

INSTRUCTIONS

1. Place the bark on your board in a stacked row down the middle.

2. Put half a row of pink macarons next to the bark and half a row of Champagne Cupcakes.

3. Fill in large empty gaps with some of the strawberries.

4. Fill in the remaining areas with pistachios and raspberries.

Mini Cheesecakes Dessert Board

Serve on a 10" × 20" cutting board

Tangy lemon cheesecakes line this board filled with fresh fruits to pair. These mini cheesecakes can be served any time of year with seasonal fruit of your choosing for a board big on fresh taste.

INGREDIENTS

6 Mini No-Bake Lemon Cheesecakes (recipe on page 151), with quartered lemon slice garnish

Whipped Cream (recipe on page 154)

3 kiwis, peeled and sliced

6 ounces raspberries

6 ounces blackberries

1 cup blueberries

16 ounces strawberries, halved

INSTRUCTIONS

1. Place cheesecakes in a line on your board.

2. Add Whipped Cream to a small ramekin or bowl in a corner of your board.

3. Place the fruits in neat rows all the way down the board, keeping them in groups.

Pavlova Dessert Board

Serve on a 13" round pizza board

An abundance of fresh fruit accompanies sweet pavlovas in this all-occasion board that is bright and fresh. The mint garnish throughout adds a lovely aroma that draws people in. This dessert will be perfect for your next gathering where you want to have something sweet to offer that is still light, airy, and gorgeous.

INGREDIENTS

Whipped Cream (recipe on page 154), make shortly before serving

10 Mini Pavlovas (recipe on page 153)

5 kiwis, peeled and sliced

2 cups cherries

6 ounces fresh blueberries

1 cup fresh blackberries

Fresh mint, to garnish

INSTRUCTIONS

1. Add Whipped Cream to a small ramekin or bowl and place slightly off-center on your board.

2. Stack some Mini Pavlovas in a section of your board and place the remaining on a plate to the side.

3. Place some kiwi halfway around the bowl of Whipped Cream and the rest along a side of the board.

4. Place two piles of cherries on opposite sides of board.

5. Place fresh blueberries in one open spot on your board and fresh blackberries in another.

6. Garnish with fresh mint for color and fragrance.

7. Instruct guests to pick a pavlova, add a dollop of whipped cream, and pile on their favorite fruits.

Chapter 4

Holiday

New Year Dessert Board

Serve on a 9" × 13" serving tray

Cheers to a new year with this sparkling board! Champagne-flavored cupcakes paired with adorably decorated sugar cookies of Champagne glassware make for the perfect toast to any New Year's celebration.

INGREDIENTS

9 Mini Champagne Cupcakes with Champagne Frosting (recipe on page 120), garnished with gold sprinkles

10 gold rock candy swizzle sticks

5.3 ounces Ferrero Rocher® chocolates, wrapped

8 ounces yogurt-covered pretzels

5–7 decorated Champagne glass/bottle sugar cookies

INSTRUCTIONS

1. Place cupcakes on your tray in a grouping toward the center.

2. Place the gold rock candy swizzle sticks in a pile on one side of tray.

3. Line up the Ferrero Rocher® chocolates in nice rows in an empty area on tray.

4. In another open area, pile on the yogurt-covered pretzels.

5. In the remaining open area, line up the decorated Champagne glass/bottle sugar cookies.

6. Serve with a side of Champagne.

Invite your guests to place a gold rock candy swizzle stick into their glass of Champagne to add color and flavor to their drink!

Valentine's Day Dessert Board

Serve on a 10" × 20" cutting board

Love is in the air with sweet treats, delectable chocolates, and heart-shaped cheese! I love this board because it has a wonderful mix of candies, chocolates, cookies, and guilt-free items like cheese, crackers, and strawberries so there is something for everyone to snack on.

INGREDIENTS

1 cup conversation heart candies

5 raspberry Linzer cookies

6 ounces heart-shaped cheddar cheese block

1 handful Triscuit crackers

2.47 ounces strawberry pocky sticks

7 pink and red rock candy swizzle sticks

6 Mini Vanilla Cupcakes (recipe on page 118) with Vanilla Buttercream Frosting (recipe on page 119), garnished with Valentine's Day–inspired sprinkles

6 Chocolate-Covered Strawberries (recipe on page 126) with pink candy melt drizzle

10 heart-shaped chocolate truffles

6 strawberry macarons

INSTRUCTIONS

1. Add some of the conversation heart candies to a small heart-shaped bowl and place on your board. Then, add a tiny heart-shaped cookie cutter next to the bowl and fill with the rest of the conversation heart candies.

2. Place the Linzer cookies around the bowl of conversation heart candies.

3. Add the heart-shaped cheddar cheese block to your board and place the Triscuit crackers in rows next to it.

4. Place the strawberry pocky sticks in a neat pile on one side of your board and the rock candy sticks in a neat pile on the other.

5. In any large open spots, add the cupcakes and chocolate-covered strawberries.

6. Fill in smaller empty spots with the heart-shaped chocolate truffles and strawberry macarons.

Mardi Gras Dessert Board

Serve on a 13" round cutting board

Serve up a board with some New Orleans style. Festive cookies set the tone for this purple, yellow, and green party board. Maybe collecting beads on Bourbon Street for Mardi Gras isn't your thing but this board still says "let's party!"

INGREDIENTS

9 ounces purple ombre coated almonds

5 purple macarons

1 handful green apple taffy

9 white and purple swirled lollipops

6 Mardi Gras–inspired sugar cookies

6 ounces candy bananas

INSTRUCTIONS

1. Add the almonds to a small ramekin or bowl and place bowl slightly off-center on your board.

2. Wrap the macarons around the bowl.

3. Place taffy in one section of your board.

4. Stack lollipops in another section.

5. Stack the sugar cookies around the curve of one side of your board.

6. Fill in the last open section of your board with candy bananas.

St. Patrick's Day Dessert Board

Serve on an 11" × 14" serving tray

Lucky you. A tray full of green and rainbow goodies is a family friendly way to celebrate this Irish holiday. Although I am all about that green beer, nothing beats sharing a few treats and a few laughs with the kids. Now, time to find out who can eat the most wasabi peas.

INGREDIENTS

6 Mini Vanilla Cupcakes (recipe on page 118) with Vanilla Buttercream Frosting (recipe on page 119), garnished with Lucky Charms marshmallows

13 mint OREO cookies

6 decorated shamrock sugar cookies

1 cup pistachios

1 cup wasabi peas

6 rainbow lollipops

5 pistachio macarons

2 cups green apple caramel corn

1 handful sour rainbow belts

1 cup dark chocolate mint swirl chocolates, unwrapped

1 handful chocolate gold coins

INSTRUCTIONS

1. Place cupcakes on one section of your tray.

2. Line one side of the board with the mint OREO Cookies.

3. Make a nice pile of sugar cookies on the other side of board.

4. Place pistachios and wasabi peas into small ramekins or bowls and spread out toward center of tray.

5. Add the rainbow lollipops into an open corner of tray.

6. Make a nice row of pistachio macarons in an open spot on tray.

7. Fill in remaining open spots with the green apple caramel corn, sour rainbow belts, and dark chocolate mint swirl chocolates.

8. Use chocolate gold coins to decorate around the board.

Easter Dessert Board

Serve on an 11" × 17" pink baking sheet

Cute bunny treats and fun egg-shaped bites add pops of color and festive décor to your next Easter gathering. This board is really easy to create. Just gather up all those fun seasonal items at your local grocery store and place on a board in groupings. Swap in different cookies or chocolates to make sure your family's favorites are presented and ready to eat.

INGREDIENTS

1 ounce green apple edible Easter grass

½ cup Robin Eggs candy

6 chocolate bunnies

12 lemon creme–filled cookies

12 Chessmen® butter cookies

3 large egg-shaped Rice Krispies Treats™ (recipe on page 127)

4 creme-filled chocolate eggs

1 cup spring trail mix with M&M's®

4–8 bunny-shaped Peeps®

1 handful fresh strawberries

1 handful fresh blackberries

INSTRUCTIONS

1. Arrange two nests with the edible Easter grass and add the Robin Eggs candy in the center of each nest.

2. Stack the chocolate bunnies in nice rows in one corner of your baking sheet.

3. Next to the chocolate bunnies, make two rows of creme cookies.

4. In another corner, add a neat row of Chessmen® butter cookies.

5. Put the egg-shaped Rice Krispies Treats™ in a large open area.

6. Pour spring trail mix with M&M's® into a small ramekin or bowl and place on your baking sheet.

7. Fill in any remaining space with bunny-shaped Peeps®, strawberries, and blackberries.

Patriotic Dessert Board

Serve on a 12" × 18" serving tray

Cue the oohs and aahs. Show your patriotism with a red, white, and blue board perfect to take to any Independence Day celebration. This patriotic board is great for both kids and adults with lots of festive, easy-to-grab snacks.

INGREDIENTS

8 Mini Vanilla Cupcakes (recipe on page 118) with Vanilla Buttercream Frosting (recipe on page 119), garnished with patriotic sprinkles

1 cup red, white, and blue M&M's®

20 red, white, and blue OREO cookies

9 red, white, and blue rock candy swizzle sticks

4 Rice Krispies Treats™ (recipe on page 127), garnished with patriotic sprinkles

4 patriotic decorated sugar cookies

1 handful red licorice

1 handful popcorn

INSTRUCTIONS

1. Add the cupcakes to two neat rows in one section of your tray.

2. Pour some red, white, and blue M&M's® in a small ramekin or bowl and place next to cupcakes.

3. Make two rows of red, white, and blue OREO cookies in two areas starting at the bowl of M&M's® and going out to the edges of your tray.

4. Place the rock candy swizzle sticks in a corner of your tray in groupings of red, white and blue.

5. Use a star-shaped cookie cutter to make star-shaped Rice Krispies Treats™ and place them next to the rock candy swizzle sticks.

6. Stack sugar cookies on the opposite corner of your tray.

7. Fill in remaining areas of tray with red licorice and popcorn.

Halloween Dessert Board

Serve on a 13" round pizza board

Liven up your Halloween party this year! A touch of fun, a touch of color, and a touch of the spooky create a bright Halloween-inspired board that you just want to dig right into! What I love about this board is how the green and orange color complement each other throughout, making a dessert that is just as fun to look at as it to eat.

INGREDIENTS

1 cup candy corn

4–6 decorated Halloween sugar cookies

6 green fudge–dipped pretzel rods ("witch fingers")

6 orange macarons

1 handful black licorice

6 green and white rock candy swizzle sticks

16 Halloween OREO cookies

½ cup gummy fangs

1 cup Mellowcreme® pumpkins

1 cup Halloween edition M&M's®

3 gummy eyeballs

INSTRUCTIONS

1. Add the candy corn to a small ramekin or bowl and place near an edge of the board.

2. Wrap the sugar cookies around the candy corn and up the edge of the board.

3. Place a stack of pretzel sticks next to the bowl of candy corn.

4. Make a neat row of orange macarons next to the pretzel sticks.

5. Place the black licorice and the rock candy swizzle sticks in stacks and slightly hang them off the edge of your board in front of the orange macarons.

6. Create a neat row of OREO cookies in an empty corner of your board.

7. Fill in any other empty spots of your board with Mellowcreme® pumpkins and M&M's®.

8. Place a few gummy eyeballs on your board for a finishing touch.

Thanksgiving Dessert Boards

Serve on 4" × 4" boards

Serve Thanksgiving dessert in style with a mini board for each of your guests. Pumpkin, apple, caramel, gingersnap, and chocolate flavors combine on this delightful little fall-inspired board.

INGREDIENTS

1 Mini Pumpkin Cheesecake, make recipe (on page 144) at least one day in advance and store in the refrigerator prior to serving and garnish with caramel sauce, whipped cream, and gingersnap cookie crumbles

3 cinnamon apple chips

1 piece caramel

1 Belgian chocolate pumpkin

3 apple slices

INSTRUCTIONS

1. Place cheesecake on a corner of your board.

2. Add apple chips in a nice row on your board.

3. Place caramel and chocolate pumpkin next to the cheesecake.

4. Fill in any remaining space with fresh apple slices.

5. Repeat steps above for all other mini boards.

Christmas Hot Cocoa Dessert Board

Serve on a 13" round cutting board

A mug filled with rich chocolatey hot cocoa warming your hands on Christmas morning as your family exchanges gifts is just about perfect. Only a hot cocoa board such as this could top that moment!

INGREDIENTS

Hot Chocolate Bombs (recipe on page 147) , garnished with a chocolate drizzle and festive sprinkles

½ cup Christmas sprinkles

6 dark chocolate pizzelles

5 peppermint Milano® cookies

4 snowman face marshmallow toppers

4 fancy candy-sprinkled marshmallow toppers

6 dark chocolate stir spoons

1 handful mini and bite-size marshmallows

6 mini peppermint candy canes, unwrapped

INSTRUCTIONS

1. Place the hot chocolate bombs in a section of your board.

2. Add Christmas sprinkles to a small ramekin or bowl and place on your board next to the hot chocolate bombs.

3. Next to the Christmas sprinkles, stack a neat row of Milano® cookies.

4. Neatly stack the dark chocolate pizzelles in a large open area of your board.

5. In another large open area of your board, stack the snowman face and fancy candy-sprinkled marshmallow toppers.

6. Place the stir spoons on your board next to the marshmallow toppers.

7. To fill up the remainder of your board, dump some mini and bite-size marshmallows alongside the stir spoons.

8. Finish your board with mini peppermint candy canes.

9. Have hot cocoa and warmed milk ready on the side with mugs to let people create their perfect cup of hot cocoa.

Christmas Dessert Board

Serve on a 17" round serving tray

Fill the holidays with love, laughter, and dazzling treats! This particular board has nothing homemade on it, which I am all about during Christmas time. Offering a Christmas board such as this is festive and spectacular, yet allows you to spend more time with your loved ones and less time in the kitchen.

INGREDIENTS

1 cup holiday cinnamon imperials

6 Christmas-decorated sugar cookies

8.5 ounces peppermint white chocolate truffles

20 OREO Joy cookies

8 holiday gourmet chocolate pretzel rods

10 ounces holiday frosted tree pretzels with yogurt flavored coating

20 ounces holiday spice gumdrops

10 ounces holiday edition milk chocolate M&M's®

INSTRUCTIONS

1. Add the holiday cinnamon imperials to a small ramekin or bowl and place off-center on your tray.

2. Wrap the sugar cookies around the imperials and up the side of the tray in a nice line.

3. Fill up an open section of your tray with the peppermint white chocolate truffles.

4. Make a row of OREOs along a side of your tray.

5. Create a pile of pretzel rods lengthwise from the imperials to the outer edge of your tray.

6. Fill the empty space in front of the OREOs with tree pretzels.

7. Fill the remaining large open section with gumdrops.

8. Finish off your tray with M&M's®.

Chapter 5

Party

Aloha Dessert Board

Serve on a 14" round serving tray

Make any pool party feel like you are in a tropical paradise with this board. A pineapple fruit dip is surrounded by fresh fruits, a bit of candy, nuts, and cookies.

INGREDIENTS

Pineapple Fruit Dip (recipe on page 122), garnished with colorful sprinkles

Chocolate-Dipped Banana Chips with Sea Salt (recipe on page 123)

4 watermelon and pineapple decorated sugar cookies

4 vanilla macarons

12 dried mango slices

½ cup sour watermelon candy slices

½ cup fresh pineapple

1 fresh dragon fruit, peeled and chopped

2 kiwi, sliced

½ cup seedless watermelon, diced

½ cup macadamia nuts

INSTRUCTIONS

1. Place dip into half a coconut shell or a small ramekin or bowl and place in middle of tray.

2. Arrange banana chips on one section of your tray.

3. Add sugar cookies and vanilla macarons.

4. Add mango slices and watermelon candy.

5. Place pineapple, watermelon, and kiwi onto tray in groupings.

6. Place dragon fruit into half a coconut shell on the side of your tray.

7. Add macadamia nuts to a small ramekin or bowl and place on your tray or on the side.

8. Decorate your tray with a couple of cocktail umbrellas for some added color and fun.

Sprinkles Dessert Board

Serve on a 13" round pizza board

Sprinkle party! Life is just more fun when sprinkles are involved. This sprinkle-filled board is perfect for a birthday party dessert table or any celebration that could use an extra pop of color and fun.

INGREDIENTS

6 ounces birthday cake cookie dough bites

6 frosted sugar cookies with rainbow sprinkles

4 frosted hot fudge sundae Pop-Tarts®, unwrapped

4 party crème filled mini cupcakes with rainbow sprinkles, unwrapped

7 rich frosted mini party donuts with rainbow sprinkles

4 ounces birthday cake marshmallows

INSTRUCTIONS

1. Add the cookie dough bites to a small ramekin or bowl and place off-center on your board.

2. Stack sugar cookies around the ramekin or bowl along the edge of your board.

3. Create a tidy row of Pop-Tarts® from the center of your board going out to an edge.

4. Stack mini cupcakes in an empty spot on your board.

5. Fill another empty section of your board with mini party donuts.

6. Fill in any remaining empty gaps on your board with marshmallow bites.

Baby Girl Dessert Board

Serve on a 12" × 18" serving tray

The celebration of a new baby is one of the most exciting moments in life. Make a baby shower special with a board of all things pink and girly! This board can easily be made in blue or any other color that the mother-to-be would love.

INGREDIENTS

7.5 ounces Wensleydale cheese with lemon and honey

½ cup pink jelly beans

6 Ferrero Rocher® chocolates

1 handful sea salt pita crackers

10 pink and white swirled lollipops

6 decorated baby girl sugar cookies

7 ounces strawberry roll wafers

1 handful pink bubble gum

1 cup pink and white marshmallows

INSTRUCTIONS

1. Cut the Wensleydale cheese into wedges and place in a section of your tray.

2. Add the pink jelly beans to a small ramekin or bowl and place in another section of your tray.

3. Place Ferrero Rocher® chocolates into pink floral-shaped candy holders and arrange three next to the Wensleydale cheese and three next to the pink jelly beans.

4. Spell out B-A-B-Y with pink plastic alphabet letters in the center of your tray.

5. Place a handful of pita crackers around the Wensleydale cheese.

6. In an open corner of your tray, stack the lollipops. These particular lollipops came with a tiny pink bow on each. If your lollipops do not have a bow, feel free to add your own.

7. In another corner, nicely stack sugar cookies.

8. In the remaining empty corner, stack strawberry roll wafers.

9. Pour pink bubble gum into the remaining large open space.

10. Fill in any extra space with pink and white marshmallows.

Galaxy Dessert Board

Proof that food can be fun! Purple and blue tones create an out-of-this-world board around a marshmallow moon. This board creation started with some really neat sprinkles that I had to do something with. Simply using the color palette from these sprinkles, a really cool board was created—maybe even my favorite.

INGREDIENTS

1 cup mini marshmallows

1 cup fresh blueberries

2 cups fresh blackberries

1 handful black licorice

6 galaxy decorated macarons

8 purple and blue rock candy swizzle sticks

7 purple and white swirled lollipops

5 mixed berry Pop-Tarts®, unwrapped

12 Doctored Up Box Cupcakes (recipe on page 116), made with purple food coloring and garnished with galaxy sprinkles

9 ounces ombre purple candy-coated almonds

1 slice white cheddar cheese

INSTRUCTIONS

1. Use a section of aluminum foil to create a moon shape on your board. Fold up the edges just slightly to create a sort of "half-moon boat" that will hold the mini marshmallows. Add marshmallows.

2. Fill in space around the marshmallows with fresh berries.

3. Place a handful of black licorice on your tray.

4. On the opposite side of your tray, line up macarons and place rock candy swizzle sticks next to them.

5. Fill in an empty space with lollipops.

6. Create a neat line of Pop-Tarts® next to black licorice.

7. Neatly place cupcakes in a large open spot on your tray, then fill in any remaining empty spots with almonds.

8. Use a 1-inch star-shaped cookie cutter on the slice of cheddar cheese to create star cutouts. Place the stars over dark areas of your tray.

Decorate a Cupcake Dessert Board

Serve on a 10" × 20" cutting board

Turn birthday cupcakes into a party activity with this board. A variety of frosting flavors and loads of toppings offer all your party guests the chance to create something they love to eat.

INGREDIENTS

18 vanilla Doctored Up Box Cupcakes (recipe on page 116), made in a mix of sizes and served in rainbow colored cupcake liners

18 chocolate Doctored Up Box Cupcakes (recipe on page 116), made in a mix of sizes and served in rainbow colored cupcake liners

16 ounces premade strawberry frosting

16 ounces premade chocolate frosting

16 ounces premade vanilla frosting

½ cup rainbow sprinkles

½ cup mini milk chocolate chips

½ cup Andes® crème de menthe chocolate chips

½ cup chopped pecans

½ cup mini M&M's®

½ cup OREO cookies, chopped

½ cup chocolate sprinkles

½ cup rainbow nonpareils

½ cup chocolate fudge sauce

½ cup unicorn sprinkles

INSTRUCTIONS

1. Place vanilla cupcakes on one side of your board and chocolate on the other.

2. Add the three different frosting flavors to pastry bags with large decorating tips and place on your board.

3. Add all the toppings to small ramekins or bowls and line them up along the sides of your board.

4. Instruct your guests to pick a cupcake, frost it with their desired frosting, and sprinkle with whatever toppings they like.

Slumber Party Dessert Board

Serve on a 11" × 14" serving tray

I can hear children's screams of excitement just looking at this picture. A memorable part of my childhood were all the slumber parties at friends' homes. I want to create those same memories for my kids with this board that is sure to inspire infectious giggles, popcorn being tossed around the room, and way too much sugar in the belly.

INGREDIENTS

1 cup smoothie Skittles®

1 cup Sour Patch Watermelon Candy

1 handful Pringles®

1 (7-ounce) bag white chocolate peanut butter cups

6 Fruit by the Foot snacks, unwrapped

6 Ring Pops®, unwrapped

1 handful bubble gum

1 (2.75-ounce) bag buttered popcorn

6 candy bracelets

INSTRUCTIONS

1. Add Skittles® to a small ramekin or bowl and place in a corner of your tray.

2. Add Sour Patch Candy to a small ramekin or bowl and place off-center on your tray.

3. Place Pringles® down the side of your tray next to the Sour Patch Candy.

4. Neatly stack white chocolate peanut butter cups to form a circle around the Skittles®.

5. Neatly stack the Fruit by the Foot snacks in the nearby corner of your tray.

6. Place two small rows of Ring Pops® next to the Pringles®.

7. Fill in the remaining open areas of your tray with bubble gum and buttered popcorn.

8. Spread out some candy bracelets to complete your tray.

Candy Jarcuterie

Serve in 4 (6-ounce) glass jars

Break all the rules with these individual jarcuteries that look and taste like a sweet candy dream. It is just like a candy board but stuffed in a convenient jar. These candy jarcuteries are great for serving at birthday parties so that each person has their own little bundle of goodies to snack on.

INGREDIENTS

1 (16-ounce) bag Skittles®

3 single packages Ultimate Party Cake Bites (8 cake bites)

8 mini powdered donuts

4 rock candy sticks

4 pink swirl lollipops, unwrapped

1 handful gummy worms

4 cupcake-shaped marshmallows

INSTRUCTIONS

1. Fill jar about halfway with Skittles®.

2. Place two of the cake bites on a toothpick and add to jar.

3. Place two mini powdered donuts on a skewer and add to jar. You may need to break off the bottom of your skewer to make it fit properly in jar.

4. Add a colorful rock candy stick and a pink swirl lollipop to jar.

5. To make the jar look nice and full, place gummy worms wherever you can squeeze them in.

6. For a finishing touch, place a marshmallow on a toothpick and add to jar.

7. Repeat steps above for other jars.

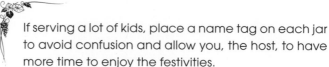

If serving a lot of kids, place a name tag on each jar to avoid confusion and allow you, the host, to have more time to enjoy the festivities.

Unicorn Dessert Board

Serve on a 17" round serving tray

This board is for the child in all of us, complete with rainbows, unicorns, and everything pink! Serve this dessert board at a unicorn princess birthday party as a great way to serve some sweet goodies and add to the décor.

INGREDIENTS

6 Mini Vanilla Cupcakes (recipe on page 118) with Vanilla Buttercream Frosting (recipe on page 119), garnished with unicorn sprinkles

1 cup pink jelly beans

1 dozen mini strawberry donuts

9 pink, blue, and purple rock candy swizzle sticks

7 decorated unicorn sugar cookies

6 unicorn magic pudding cups

1 jumbo rainbow swirl marshmallow

2 cups rainbow marshmallows

INSTRUCTIONS

1. Place cupcakes down the side of one quadrant of your board.

2. Pour pink jelly beans into a small ramekin or bowl and place toward the center of your board.

3. Fill a section of your board with mini donuts.

4. Stack rock candy swizzle sticks next to the donuts and out to the edge of the board.

5. Stack sugar cookies on the other side of the donuts.

6. Line up the pudding cups in a large empty area of your board.

7. Fill in the rest of your board with marshmallows.

Sunday Football Dessert Board

Serve on a 13" round cutting board

Show your creative side this coming Super Bowl with a board dedicated to football. Let's be honest, most of us just show up for the food anyway, so make something memorable for all your friends and family.

INGREDIENTS

7 ounces popcorn-flavored M&M's®

7 chocolate Doctored Up Box Cupcakes (recipe on page 116), garnished with green frosting and a plastic football

9 Chocolate-Covered Strawberries (recipe on page 126), garnished with white chocolate lace

12 Chocolate-Dipped Pretzel Rods (recipe on page 124), garnished with white chocolate lace

1 cup caramel apple popcorn

1 cup yogurt-covered pretzels

½ cup yogurt-covered raisins

INSTRUCTIONS

1. Pour M&M's® into a small ramekin or bowl and place on board toward the center.

2. Fill a section of your board with cupcakes.

3. Add chocolate-covered strawberries to another section of your board.

4. Fill a large open area of your board with a stack of chocolate-dipped pretzel rods.

5. Fill in any remaining open areas of your board with caramel apple popcorn, yogurt-covered pretzels, and yogurt-covered raisins.

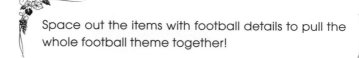

Space out the items with football details to pull the whole football theme together!

Mermaid Dessert Board

Serve on a 13" round pizza board

Sparkling cookies inspired this beautiful dessert board filled with purples, blues, and greens. This is the perfect board to add a little something special to a mermaid-themed party without a lot of fuss.

INGREDIENTS

8 Mini Vanilla Cupcakes (recipe on page 118) with Vanilla Buttercream Frosting (recipe on page 119), garnished with mermaid sprinkles

4 bluish-green mermaid pudding cups

5 strawberry unicorn cakes

4 mermaid-inspired sugar cookies

6 rock candy swizzle sticks in white, blue, and purple

1 cup sparkling mythical creature cookies

INSTRUCTIONS

1. Add mini cupcakes to a large section of your board.

2. Add mermaid pudding cups to another section.

3. Next to the mini cupcakes, create a stack of unicorn cakes followed by a row of mermaid-inspired sugar cookies. You may need to rearrange some of the mini cupcakes so that half of your board is completely filled and colorful.

4. Stack the rock candy swizzle sticks in another large open section of your board.

5. Fill in any remaining gaps on your board with sparkling mythical creature cookies.

Baseball Dessert Board

Serve on a 13" round pizza board

Any end-of-season baseball gathering, World Series get-together, or baseball-themed birthday party will benefit from this dessert board. This board mixes items that don't necessarily go together like licorice and sunflower seeds into a coherent spread that pulls together beautifully. No matter how old you are, any baseball fanatic will go bananas over this one.

INGREDIENTS

1 cup sunflower seeds in shell

16 ounces red licorice

8 ounces sour gumballs in baseball design

5–7 baseball-themed sugar cookies

2 (2-ounce) packets bubble gum chew

5 red rock candy swizzle sticks

INSTRUCTIONS

1. Add the sunflower seeds to a small ramekin or bowl and place toward the edge of your board.

2. Place red licorice on your board pointing from the sunflower seeds going out to the board's edge.

3. Place sour gumballs next to sunflower seeds.

4. Stack sugar cookies on each side of the red licorice.

5. Place packets of bubble gum chew in the open space between sugar cookies and sunflower seeds.

6. Stack red rock candy swizzle sticks between sour gumballs and sugar cookies.

7. Add some extra sour gumballs throughout the board so that there is baseball decoration everywhere.

Candy Dessert Board

Serve on a 10" × 20" cutting board

A dessert board fully dedicated to fun with candy! Ring pops®, drinkable candy, popping candy, rainbow lollipops, marshmallow cones, emoji chocolates, and candy buttons will surely bring out the inner child in us all.

INGREDIENTS

½ cup assorted jelly beans

½ cup M&M's®

4 (.33-ounce) Pop Rocks® popping candy envelopes

.5 ounce candy button sheets

5 marshmallow candy cones

5 rainbow unicorn lollipops, unwrapped

9 ounces twisted rainbow punch SweeTART™ ropes

6 Ring Pops®, unwrapped

1 handful Jolly Rancher hard candies

1 handful sour gummy worms

2 (1.39-ounce) Nik-L-Nip mini drinks

6 chocolate foil emojis

INSTRUCTIONS

1. Place assorted jelly beans and M&M's® into small ramekins or bowls and spread them out on your board.

2. Stack the Pop Rocks® toward the center and out to the edge of your board.

3. Cut the candy button sheets into sections and spread out along the edges of board.

4. Fan out marshmallow candy cones in a corner of your board.

5. Place lollipops next to the marshmallow candy cones in a tidy stack.

6. Make a stack of the SweeTART™ ropes in a large open spot.

7. Place Ring Pops® in rows in an open area in the center of your board.

8. Fill in remaining space on board with Jolly Rancher hard candies and sour gummy worms.

9. Finish your board with some Nik-L-Nip mini drinks and chocolate foil emojis.

Chapter 6

Accompaniments

Jam and Cream Cheese Hand Pies

Servings: 6
Total Time: 45 minutes

These mini handheld pies are tasty and adorable. You will be surprised just how easy these pies are to make. A store-bought crust and a few basic ingredients make a really fun pie to share with friends.

INGREDIENTS

2 homemade or store-bought pie crusts, room temperature

6 tablespoons cream cheese, room temperature

1 teaspoon granulated sugar

6 teaspoons jam of choice

Sparkling sugar, to garnish

INSTRUCTIONS

1. Preheat oven to 400°F.

2. Use a 3.5-inch biscuit cutter to cut six circles from both pie crusts for a total of 12 mini circular pie crusts. Half will be used as the bottoms and half will be used as the tops of the pies.

3. In a mixing bowl, beat the cream cheese with granulated sugar until creamy.

4. Add cream cheese filling to six of the mini circular pie crusts, then add jam of choice on top.

5. Dip a finger in water and spread on the outside edges of those same six mini circular pie crusts. The water will help adhere the bottom and top of each pie together.

6. Immediately top the six filled mini crusts with the other six crusts.

7. Use a fork to gently press in the edges of each pie.

8. Take a knife and make a slit on top of each pie so that it vents in the oven.

9. Place pies on baking sheet and bake for 15 minutes or until the edges begin to brown.

10. Once baked, garnish each pie with a sprinkle of sparkling sugar and let cool.

Doctored Up Box Cupcakes

Servings: 24 regular sized cupcakes
Total Time: 30 minutes for regular, 20 minutes for mini

Some extra egg, whole milk, and butter sure does go a long way in a store-bought box of cake mix for moist, delicious cupcakes. Make baking easier with this jazzed-up box cake mix and get that fresh-from-the-bakery taste every time.

INGREDIENTS

1 (15-ounce) box cake mix of choice

1 cup whole milk

4 eggs

¾ cup unsalted butter, melted

Frosting of choice

INSTRUCTIONS

1. Preheat oven to 350°F.

2. Add cake mix to a large mixing bowl.

3. Add in milk, eggs, and melted butter and whisk until batter is smooth.

4. Add cupcake liners to a cupcake pan and fill each cup ¾ full.

5. Bake for 20 minutes and let cool.

6. Frost cupcakes and decorate as desired.

Follow the same instructions for mini cupcakes but bake for only 10 minutes in a mini cupcake pan with mini cupcake liners.

Mini Vanilla Cupcakes

Servings: 50 cupcakes
Total Time: 20 minutes

These mini vanilla cupcakes are made with basic ingredients to create moist, fluffy bites of yum. These cupcakes are my go-to for almost any dessert board.

INGREDIENTS

1⅔ cups all-purpose flour or 1¾ cup cake flour

1 cup granulated sugar

½ teaspoon salt

¼ teaspoon baking soda

1½ teaspoons baking powder

¾ cup unsalted butter, melted

½ tablespoon vanilla extract

½ cup whole milk

½ cup plain or vanilla full-fat Greek yogurt

3 egg whites

INSTRUCTIONS

1. Preheat oven to 350°F.

2. Combine dry cupcake ingredients in a large mixing bowl. Whisk together and set to the side.

3. In a separate bowl, whisk together the melted butter, vanilla extract, whole milk, and Greek yogurt. Combine with the dry ingredients and whisk well.

4. Use a hand mixer to beat egg whites until a foam is formed. Fold this foam into your cupcake batter.

5. Place cupcake liners into a mini cupcake pan and fill each ⅔ full of batter.

6. Bake for 10 minutes and let cool. Frost and decorate when cupcakes are at room temperature.

Vanilla Buttercream Frosting

Servings: 32
Total Time: 5 minutes

A simple frosting recipe is a necessity for any home cook. This Vanilla Buttercream Frosting comes together quickly and pipes easily to add a sweet touch to any cupcake.

INGREDIENTS

½ cup unsalted butter, softened

1 teaspoon vanilla extract

1 pinch salt

2+ cups confectioners' sugar

½+ tablespoon heavy whipping cream

Food coloring (optional)

INSTRUCTIONS

1. Place softened butter into a mixing bowl and use a hand or stand mixer to beat butter until creamy.

2. Add in vanilla extract and salt.

3. Slowly add in confectioners' sugar and heavy whipping cream in increments. Two cups of confectioner sugar and ½ tablespoon heavy whipping cream is a good starting point but if the frosting seems too thick, add more cream, or if it seems too runny, add more sugar until you have a good pipeable frosting consistency.

4. Place frosting into a pastry bag with a large frosting decorating tip.

5. Pipe each cupcake.

Food coloring can be used to change frosting color.

Champagne Cupcakes with Champagne Buttercream Frosting

Servings: 24 cupcakes
Total Time: 35 minutes for regular, 25 minutes for mini

A bit of Champagne goes a long way in basic cake mix for a fluffy and flavorful little treat. Any sparkling wine may be used in this recipe.

INGREDIENTS

Champagne Cupcakes

3 egg whites

1 box white cake mix

⅓ cup unsalted butter, melted

1¼ cups alcoholic or nonalcoholic sparkling wine (use pink rosé sparkling wine for pink Champagne cupcakes)

1 dab red food coloring for pink Champagne cupcakes

Champagne Frosting

½ cup unsalted butter, room temperature

½ cup vegetable shortening

¼ cup alcoholic or nonalcoholic sparkling wine (use pink rosé sparkling wine for pink Champagne cupcakes)

4 cups powdered sugar

1 dab red food coloring for pink Champagne cupcakes

INSTRUCTIONS

1. Preheat oven to 350°F.

2. In a large mixing bowl, add egg whites, white cake mix, ⅓ cup unsalted butter, and 1¼ cups sparkling wine. Mix well.

3. If making pink Champagne cupcakes, add a dab of red food coloring and mix in using a spatula. Start with just a little food coloring and add more if needed.

4. Place cupcake liners in a cupcake pan and fill each cup ¾ full of cupcake mixture.

5. Bake for 20 minutes and let cool.

6. In a large mixing bowl, add ½ cup unsalted butter, vegetable shortening, sparkling wine, and powdered sugar. Use a hand mixer to thoroughly mix.

7. If making pink champagne cupcakes, add a dab of red food coloring to frosting and stir color in completely.

8. Place frosting in decorating bag with tip of choice and frost and decorate each cupcake as desired.

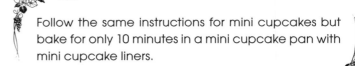

Follow the same instructions for mini cupcakes but bake for only 10 minutes in a mini cupcake pan with mini cupcake liners.

Fruit Dip

Servings: 8
Total Time: 5 minutes

This go-to recipe consists of only four basic ingredients and will pair with any fruit. I like this dip because it adds something cool and creamy to a bite of sweet, fresh fruit.

INGREDIENTS

1 cup heavy whipping cream

½ cup confectioners' sugar

1 teaspoon vanilla extract

8 ounces cream cheese, room temperature

INSTRUCTIONS

1. Place a large mixing bowl and hand mixer beaters into the freezer for 20 minutes to chill.

2. Once cold, remove the mixing bowl and beaters from the freezer and add the heavy cream, confectioners' sugar, and vanilla extract to cold bowl.

3. Beat for about 7 minutes until stiff peaks form. A stiff peak is achieved when the beaters are removed from whipped cream and the whipped cream does not flop over.

4. In a separate bowl, add softened cream cheese and beat until creamy.

5. Add the whipped topping to cream cheese and quickly beat to combine ingredients.

Pineapple Fruit Dip

Servings: 8
Total Time: 7 minutes

An easy variation of a classic fruit dip with added sweetness and flavor from pineapple.

INGREDIENTS

1 cup heavy whipping cream

½ cup confectioners' sugar

1 teaspoon vanilla extract

8 ounces cream cheese, room temperature

8 ounces canned crushed pineapple, strained

INSTRUCTIONS

1. Place mixing bowl and hand mixer beaters into the freezer for 20 minutes to chill.

2. Once cold, remove the mixing bowl and beaters from the freezer and add the heavy cream, confectioners' sugar, and vanilla extract to cold bowl.

3. Beat for about 7 minutes until stiff peaks form. A stiff peak is achieved when the beaters are removed from whipped cream and the whipped cream does not flop over.

4. In a separate bowl, add softened cream cheese and beat until creamy.

5. Add the whipped topping to cream cheese and quickly beat to combine ingredients.

6. Finally, fold in strained pineapple.

Chocolate-Dipped Banana Chips with Sea Salt

Servings: 8
Total Time: 15 minutes

Sweet banana chips dipped in creamy dark chocolate are balanced with a sprinkle of sea salt for a tasty little treat that is surprisingly quick and simple. I love snacking on these banana chips when I feel like having something sweet and chocolatey that's not too heavy or overindulgent. These just hit the spot.

INGREDIENTS

1 cup dark chocolate melting wafers

2 cups banana chips

Coarse sea salt, to garnish

INSTRUCTIONS

1. Melt chocolate wafers in a microwave-safe container or mug in 30 second increments, stirring between, until fully melted.

2. Dip each banana chip halfway into melted chocolate.

3. Place on parchment paper to set and garnish with sea salt.

Chocolate-Dipped Pretzel Rods

Servings: 24
Total Time: 15 minutes

This easy treat to make and eat is salty *and* sweet. Decorate as you wish to fit the theme of any dessert board.

INGREDIENTS

10 ounces dark chocolate melting wafers, divided

2 dozen pretzel rods

Extra toppings of choice (sprinkles, crushed cookies, extra chocolate, crushed candy canes, etc.), to garnish

INSTRUCTIONS

1. Lay parchment paper out.

2. Place melting wafers into a microwave-safe tall, narrow glass. Microwave in 30 second increments, stirring between, until fully melted.

3. Dip each pretzel rod into melted chocolate, then place onto parchment paper.

4. If adding extra toppings, garnish immediately before chocolate sets.

Variation

Football Chocolate-Dipped Pretzel Rods: Once the chocolate has set, melt ½ cup white candy melts and place into a piping or resealable bag. Cut a small opening in corner of bag and pipe lines onto each pretzel in a football lace pattern.

Chocolate Hummus

Servings: 8
Total Time: 12 minutes

This creamy, chocolaty, guilt-free dip will keep you coming back for more. The words healthy and dessert do not often go together but this bean-based dip is just that and you won't believe how delicious it is!

INGREDIENTS

1 (15-ounce) can black beans, drained

2 tablespoons baking cocoa powder

3 tablespoons organic maple syrup

1 teaspoon vanilla extract

1 pinch sea salt

½ cup milk chocolate chips, melted

Dark chocolate sauce, to garnish

Mini milk chocolate chips, to garnish

INSTRUCTIONS

1. Add black beans, cocoa powder, maple syrup, vanilla extract, and sea salt to food processor. Blend for 1 minute.

2. Place the chocolate chips into a microwave-safe container and microwave in 30 second increments until completely melted, then pour into food processor.

3. Blend ingredients together to form a creamy hummus. If hummus needs thinning out, add a teaspoon of water or more as needed to create desired consistency.

4. Place hummus into a bowl and garnish with dark chocolate sauce and mini chocolate chips.

Chocolate-Covered Strawberries

Servings: 12 strawberries
Total Time: 12 minutes

The bittersweet chocolate combined with the fresh, sweet strawberry creates luscious and beautiful little treats to serve for any occasion.

INGREDIENTS

1 cup dark chocolate melting wafers

12 fresh strawberries, rinsed

¼ cup candy melts in color of choice (optional)

INSTRUCTIONS

1. Lay parchment paper out.

2. Melt dark chocolate melting wafers in a microwave-safe container or mug in 30 second increments, stirring between, until completely melted.

3. Holding each strawberry by the stem, dip in melted chocolate and place on parchment paper to set.

4. If using candy melts, melt them in a microwave-safe container or mug in 30 second increments, stirring between, until fully melted.

5. Place candy melts into piping or resealable bag with a small slit and drizzle over each strawberry.

6. Serve once strawberries are set.

Variation

Football Chocolate-Dipped Pretzel Rods: Once the chocolate has set, melt ½ cup white candy melts and place into a piping or resealable bag. Cut a small opening in corner of bag and pipe lines onto each strawberry in a football lace pattern.

Rice Krispies Treats™

Servings: 12
Total Time: 10 minutes

A classic Rice Krispies Treats™ recipe should be in everyone's dessert arsenal. Yeah, store-bought would be fine, but there is something about the soft, gooey, homemade kind that cannot be beat.

INGREDIENTS

3 tablespoons unsalted butter

4 cups miniature marshmallows

6 cups rice cereal

Sprinkles of choice, to garnish

INSTRUCTIONS

1. In a large saucepan, melt butter.

2. Remove pan from heat, add marshmallows, and stir until melted.

3. Stir in rice cereal.

4. Press into a 9" × 13" pan coated with nonstick spray.

5. Garnish with sprinkles of choice.

6. Let cool and cut into squares or shapes.

Chocolate Fondue Dip

Servings: 10
Total Time: 12 minutes

Make dessert fun with this shareable dip of high-quality chocolate melted with some butter, heavy cream, and vanilla extract. Easy to make and easy to share.

INGREDIENTS

10 ounces high-quality semisweet chocolate bar, chopped

1 tablespoon unsalted butter

½ cup heavy cream

½ teaspoon vanilla extract

INSTRUCTIONS

1. Combine the chocolate, butter, heavy cream, and vanilla extract in a heatproof bowl and set it over a pot of simmering water. Make sure the water does not touch the bottom of the bowl. Stir the mixture over the heat until just melted and smooth.

2. Place into a serving bowl and serve immediately.

Chocolate Cheesecake Dip

Servings: 6
Total Time: 12 minutes

This smooth and creamy chocolate dip is easy to share and delightful for dipping cookies or fresh fruits into. The cream cheese gives this dip that cheesecake-like flavor and the milk chocolate adds a subtle flavor that is just really enjoyable.

INGREDIENTS

4 ounces cream cheese, softened

½ cup heaving whipping cream

½ cup confectioners' sugar

½ teaspoon vanilla extract

½ cup milk chocolate chips

Mini milk chocolate chips, to garnish

INSTRUCTIONS

1. Place mixing bowl and beaters in freezer to get cold while cream cheese softens.

2. Once cold, remove the mixing bowl and beaters from freezer and add the heavy cream, confectioners' sugar, and vanilla extract to cold bowl.

3. Beat for about 7 minutes until stiff peaks form. A stiff peak is achieved when the beaters are removed from whipped cream and the whipped cream does not flop over.

4. In a separate mixing bowl, beat the cream cheese until smooth. Add the whipped cream and mix together.

5. Melt the chocolate chips in a microwave-safe container in 30 second increments, stirring between, until fully melted.

6. Add the chocolate to cream cheese mixture and beat until smooth. Do not overbeat.

7. Place chocolate cheesecake dip into a serving bowl. Garnish with mini chocolate chips and serve immediately.

Waffles

Servings: 6
Total: 10 minutes

Waffles are one of my favorite weekend brunch items. This recipe makes soft, fluffy waffles with a nice hint of cinnamon that can be topped with whatever you wish, from fresh fruit to maple syrup.

INGREDIENTS

2 egg whites

2¼ cups all-purpose flour

1 tablespoon baking powder

1 tablespoon confectioners' sugar

½ teaspoon salt

½ teaspoon ground cinnamon

1 teaspoon vanilla extract

½ cup vegetable oil

2 cups whole milk

INSTRUCTIONS

1. In a small mixing bowl, use a hand or stand mixer to beat 2 egg whites to a soft peak or until they are white and fluffy. Set to the side.

2. In a large mixing bowl, add all other ingredients and whisk until blended.

3. Fold in the egg whites.

4. Warm up your waffle maker and add ½ cup batter. Cook 3 to 4 minutes or as per your waffle maker's instructions.

S'mores Snack Mix

Servings: 8
Total Time: 3 minutes

This sweet snack mix is made with the beloved flavors of s'mores: Golden Grahams™ cereal, Teddy Grahams, soft mini marshmallows, and dark chocolate. I also love the addition of peanuts for that saltiness and extra crunch.

INGREDIENTS

½ cup Golden Grahams™ cereal

½ cup Teddy Grahams

½ cup mini marshmallows

¼ cup salted peanuts

½ cup mini dark chocolate chips

INSTRUCTIONS

1. Place all ingredients into a medium sized mixing bowl.

2. Mix together and serve.

S'mores Dip

Servings: 8
Total Time: 10 minutes

This warm and gooey dip made with only two ingredients makes for a fun spin on the classic s'mores dessert.

INGREDIENTS

1 cup semisweet chocolate chips

1 cup marshmallows

INSTRUCTIONS

1. Preheat oven to 425°F.

2. Place semisweet chocolate chips on the bottom of a miniature .5 quart Dutch oven and top with marshmallows.

3. Bake for 5 minutes or until the marshmallows brown slightly and get gooey.

4. Serve warm.

Pumpkin Cheesecake Dip

Servings: 16
Total Time: 15 minutes

The perfect fall favorite flavor of pumpkin mixed into this dippable, creamy dip is something to really rave about.

INGREDIENTS

1 cup heavy cream

8 ounces cream cheese, softened

1 cup confectioner's sugar

1 (3.4-ounce) packet vanilla instant pudding

½ teaspoon pumpkin pie spice

INSTRUCTIONS

1. Place beaters from hand mixer and a mixing bowl into the freezer to chill.

2. Once cold, remove the beaters and mixing bowl from freezer and beat the heavy cream for about 7 minutes until stiff peaks form. A stiff peak is achieved when the beaters are removed from whipped cream and the whipped cream does not flop over.

3. To another mixing bowl, add cream cheese and confectioners' sugar and beat until creamy.

4. Add in the pudding and pumpkin pie spice and beat again.

5. Fold the whipped cream into the cream cheese mixture until fully mixed.

6. Serve immediately.

Mini Bundt Cakes

Servings: 12
Total Time: 45 minutes

These sweet Bundt cakes are fluffy, moist, and personal sized with a slight hint of orange flavoring. That slight hint of orange has a nice aroma and goes so nicely with some fresh fruits on top.

INGREDIENTS

1 cup unsalted butter, softened

1⅔ cups granulated sugar

4 eggs, room temperature

½ cup sour cream

½ teaspoon vanilla extract

1 tablespoon orange juice

Zest of 1 small orange

2 teaspoons baking powder

¼ teaspoon baking soda

½ teaspoon salt

2¾ cups all-purpose flour

¾ cup buttermilk

INSTRUCTIONS

1. Preheat oven to 350°F.

2. In a large mixing bowl, use a hand or stand mixer to beat the butter and granulated sugar together until smooth.

3. Add eggs in one at a time and beat.

4. Add in the sour cream, vanilla extract, orange juice, and zest and beat again.

5. Add in the baking powder, baking soda, and salt.

6. In four batches, alternate adding in the flour and the buttermilk until you have a nice, consistent batter.

7. Spray a mini fluted tube pan (I recommend silicone) with nonstick spray.

8. Pour batter into ¾ of each cup and bake for 30 minutes.

9. Let cool for 15 minutes, then release each mini Bundt cake from the pan.

Icing

Servings: 16
Total Time: 3 minutes

Add a little drizzle of this icing over cake for some added sweetness and moisture with only three ingredients of confectioners' sugar, milk, and vanilla extract.

INGREDIENTS

1 cup confectioners' sugar

½ teaspoon vanilla extract

1 tablespoon milk

INSTRUCTIONS

1. Whisk the confectioners' sugar, vanilla extract, and milk together in a small bowl. If the icing looks like it thinned out a bit, add a pinch more sugar and whisk again.

2. Drizzle over desserts.

Caramel Apple Dip

Servings: 8
Total Time: 5 minutes

Calling all caramel lovers! This three-ingredient dip is packed with flavor and possibilities. Great to serve with dessert bites like gingersnap cookies or even healthier sliced apples.

INGREDIENTS

8 ounces cream cheese, softened

¼ cup confectioners' sugar

¼ cup caramel sauce + extra for garnish

Chopped HEATH candies, for garnish

INSTRUCTIONS

1. Place the softened cream cheese in a mixing bowl with confectioners' sugar and caramel sauce.

2. Beat the mixture until smooth and creamy. Transfer to a small bowl.

3. Drizzle the top with more caramel sauce and garnish with chopped HEATH candies.

4. Serve.

Peanut Butter Dip

Servings: 16
Total Time: 5 minutes

Creamy and oh-so-peanut-buttery! Creamy peanut butter mixes in perfectly with cream cheese and fluffy homemade whipped cream in this dip that you will not be able to stop eating.

INGREDIENTS

1 cup heavy cream

8 ounces cream cheese, softened

1 cup creamy peanut butter

½ cup confectioners' sugar

1 teaspoon vanilla extract

Mini semisweet chocolate chips, for garnish

INSTRUCTIONS

1. Place beaters from hand mixer and a mixing bowl into the freezer to chill.

2. Once cold, remove the beaters and mixing bowl from freezer and beat heavy cream for about 7 minutes until stiff peaks form. A stiff peak is achieved when the beaters are removed from whipped cream and the whipped cream does not flop over.

3. To another mixing bowl, add softened cream cheese with creamy peanut butter, confectioners' sugar, and vanilla extract. Beat until creamy.

4. Fold the whipped cream into the cream cheese mixture until fully mixed.

5. Place into a small bowl and garnish with mini semisweet chocolate chips.

6. Serve immediately.

Mint Chocolate Dip

Servings: 8
Total Time: 5 minutes

A cool minty flavor is whipped into a creamy, dippable bowl of deliciousness. Serve with chocolate cookies for that beloved mint chocolate food combination.

INGREDIENTS

4 ounces cream cheese, softened

½ cup heaving whipping cream

½ cup confectioner's sugar

2 teaspoons peppermint extract

½ cup white chocolate chips

Chopped Andes® crème de menthe chocolates, for garnish

INSTRUCTIONS

1. Place mixing bowl and beaters in freezer to get cold while cream cheese softens.

2. Once cold, remove the mixing bowl and beaters from freezer and beat the heavy cream, confectioners' sugar, and peppermint extract for about 7 minutes until stiff peaks form. A stiff peak is achieved when the beaters are removed from whipped cream and the whipped cream does not flop over.

3. In a separate mixing bowl, beat the cream cheese until smooth. Add in the whipped cream and mix together.

4. Melt the chocolate chips in a microwave-safe container in 30 second increments, stirring between, until fully melted.

5. Add the melted chocolate to cream cheese mixture and beat until smooth. Do not overbeat.

6. Place dip into a serving bowl and garnish with chopped Andes® crème de menthe chocolates.

No-Churn Vanilla Ice Cream

Makes: 1½ quarts
Total Time: 5 minutes + 6 hour setting time

Forget store-bought ice cream. Make your own without an ice cream maker. You won't believe how simple this no-churn ice cream is to make! The ice cream will turn out smooth and with just the right amount of vanilla flavor. Try this ice cream with some fun additions like crushed cookies, peanut butter cups, or fruit purees.

INGREDIENTS

2 teaspoons vanilla extract

14 ounces condensed milk

16 ounces heavy whipping cream

INSTRUCTIONS

1. Place a mixing bowl and beaters into freezer to chill for 30 minutes.

2. In a second mixing bowl, whisk vanilla extract and condensed milk.

3. Once cold, remove chilled bowl and beaters from freezer and beat heavy cream for about 7 minutes until stiff peaks form. A stiff peak is achieved when the beaters are removed from whipped cream and the whipped cream does not flop over.

4. Fold the condensed milk mixture into the whipped cream.

5. Pour the ice cream mixture into an ice cream tub.

6. Cover and freeze for 6+ hours.

Mini Pumpkin Cheesecakes

Servings: 6
Total Time: 15 minutes + 2 hour setting time

Dessert portioned just right for a few joyful bites of smooth pumpkin cheesecake. Top with caramel sauce, whipped cream, and some gingersnap cookie crumbles.

INGREDIENTS

8 ounces cream cheese, softened

½ cup granulated sugar

1 egg

½ teaspoon vanilla extract

1 teaspoon pumpkin pie spice

¾ cup pure pumpkin puree

20 gingersnap cookies + extra for garnish

1 tablespoon unsalted butter, melted

Caramel sauce, for garnish

Whipped cream, for garnish

INSTRUCTIONS

1. Place cream cheese in a mixing bowl with the granulated sugar. Use a hand or stand mixer to beat until smooth and creamy.

2. Add in egg, vanilla extract, and pumpkin pie spice and beat again.

3. Add the pumpkin puree and beat until puree is fully mixed in. Set aside.

4. Put the gingersnap cookies into a food processor and blend until fully crushed.

5. In a separate small ramekin or bowl, mix melted butter with crushed gingersnap cookies.

6. Place 6 cupcake liners inside a cupcake pan and equally fill each cup with the crushed gingersnap cookie mixture. Use the back of a spoon to press mixture down gently to form a crust.

7. Equally fill each cup with the cream cheese mixture.

8. Place cheesecakes into refrigerator to set for a minimum of two hours.

9. Remove from refrigerator and take cheesecakes out of cupcake liners.

10. Garnish with a dollop of caramel sauce, whipped cream, and crushed gingersnap cookies.

Hot Chocolate Bombs

Servings: 6
Total Time: 30 minutes

Add some decadence to your mug with these homemade hot chocolate bombs. Chocolate spheres are stuffed with hot cocoa mix, marshmallows, and sprinkles. Just place one into your mug and pour warm milk on top to watch the sphere burst open!

INGREDIENTS

10 ounces milk chocolate melting wafers + extra for garnish

12 tablespoons hot cocoa mix (2 tablespoons per hot chocolate bomb)

1 teaspoon sprinkles + extra for garnish

1 tablespoon mini marshmallows

48 ounces milk (8 ounces per chocolate bomb)

Whipped cream, for garnish

INSTRUCTIONS

1. In a microwave-safe container, melt the milk chocolate wafers in 30 second intervals, stirring between, until completely melted.

2. Pour the melted chocolate in even portions into medium-sized, 2½-inch sphere molds. Use the back of a spoon to manipulate the melted chocolate up the sides.

3. Place the molds in the freezer for 20 minutes to set before continuing to next step.

4. Once set, carefully release the chocolate from the molds.

5. Set up a working station with your spheres, cocoa mix, sprinkles, marshmallows, and a hot plate. (For your hot plate, microwave a ceramic plate for a minute or until it is almost too hot to touch.) Be careful!

6. Work quickly to assemble each mold into a round sphere with all the delicious goodies inside and place each sphere onto the hot plate to even out the edges.

7. Add cocoa mix, sprinkles, and mini marshmallows inside each half sphere, then place two half spheres together and move to parchment paper.

8. Repeat until all 6 spheres are complete.

9. Finish off each sphere with a little decoration. Melt down a few more chocolate wafers and drizzle over each hot chocolate bomb. Immediately add a pinch of sprinkles to each.

10. To serve, place a hot chocolate bomb into a mug and pour hot milk on top. Stir well and top with whipped cream.

Rose and Pistachio Chocolate Bark

Servings: 12
Total Time: 10 minutes

This chocolate bark with bits of crunchy, salty pistachios and a light, floral note of rose is one of my favorites. Just one square subdues those chocolate cravings.

INGREDIENTS

10 ounces high-quality chocolate bar, chopped

⅓ cup salted pistachios, chopped

1 tablespoon dried rose buds and petals, chopped

INSTRUCTIONS

1. Spread out a piece of parchment paper.

2. Place the chocolate chunks in a heatproof bowl and set it over a pot of simmering water. Make sure the water does not touch the bottom of the bowl. Stir the mixture over the heat until just melted and smooth.

3. Carefully pour the chocolate over your parchment paper. Note that the bowl will be very hot.

4. Use a spatula to smooth out the chocolate into a very thin layer, about ⅛-inch thick, in a rectangular shape.

5. Immediately sprinkle the pistachios and dried rose buds and petals on top.

6. Let cool and set completely before cutting into squares.

7. Serve.

Cranberry and Salted Peanut Chocolate Bark

Servings: 12
Total Time: 10 minutes

Chocolate with crunchy peanuts, tart fried cranberries, and a touch sea salt sprinkled over top. This chocolate has a crave-able combination with sweet, tart, and salty notes that make taste buds happy.

INGREDIENTS

10 ounces high-quality chocolate bar, chopped

¼ cup dried cranberries, chopped

½ cup unsalted peanuts, chopped

Coarse sea salt, for garnish

INSTRUCTIONS

1. Spread out a piece of parchment paper.

2. Place the chocolate chunks in a heatproof bowl and set it over a pot of simmering water. Make sure the water does not touch the bottom of the bowl. Stir the mixture over the heat until just melted and smooth.

3. Carefully pour the chocolate over the parchment paper. Note that the bowl will be very hot.

4. Use a spatula to smooth out the chocolate in a very thin layer, about ⅛-inch thick, in a rectangular shape.

5. Immediately sprinkle the dried cranberries and peanuts on top and garnish with coarse sea salt.

6. Let cool and set completely before cutting into squares.

7. Serve.

Mini No-Bake Lemon Cheesecakes

Serves: 6
Total Time: 20 minutes + 2 hour setting time

Cheesecake is probably my favorite dessert because there are so many possibilities! I particularly love creating no-bake cheesecakes because even the subtlest of flavors add something extra special. These cheesecakes have a simple filling mixed with a bit of sour lemon and put into tiny graham cracker crusts for a slightly tangy personal dessert that is fresh and pleasing. I especially like this recipe paired with whipped cream and fresh fruits.

INGREDIENTS

1½ cups heavy cream

16 ounces cream cheese, softened

4 tablespoons confectioners' sugar

½ teaspoon vanilla extract

1 tablespoon lemon juice

Zest of 1 lemon

2 tablespoons sour cream

6 mini graham cracker crusts

INSTRUCTIONS

1. Place beaters from hand mixer and a mixing bowl into the freezer to chill for 30 minutes.

2. Once cold, remove the beaters and mixing bowl from freezer and beat the cup of heavy cream for about 7 minutes until stiff peaks form. A stiff peak is achieved when the beaters are removed from whipped cream and the whipped cream does not flop over.

3. Place the softened cream cheese in a mixing bowl with the confectioners' sugar. Use a hand or stand mixer to beat until smooth and creamy.

4. Add in the vanilla extract, lemon juice, zest, and sour cream and beat until fully mixed.

5. Fold in the whipped cream until fully mixed.

6. Place filling into each graham cracker crust.

7. Refrigerate for a minimum of 2 hours before serving.

Mini Pavlovas

Serves: 12
Total Time: 2 hours

Pavlovas are a delicate meringue-based dessert that have a crisp, airy outside layer and a marshmallow layer on the inside. Add some homemade whipped cream to the tops. These Mini Pavlovas pair perfectly with fresh fruits and a sweet drizzle of honey or jam.

INGREDIENTS

6 egg whites

1 pinch salt

1¼ cups superfine sugar

2 teaspoons cornstarch

1 teaspoon white wine vinegar

½ teaspoon vanilla extract

Whipped cream, for garnish

Fresh fruits, for garnish

Honey or jam, for garnish

Mint, for garnish

INSTRUCTIONS

1. Preheat oven to 225°F.

2. Beat egg whites in a stand or hand mixer. Add salt and slowly add sugar 1 tablespoon at a time and beat for 10 minutes.

3. In your last minute of mixing, add the cornstarch, white wine vinegar, and vanilla extract.

4. Place mixture into a pastry bag, cut tip, and pipe 12 little "nests" onto a silicone baking mat set on a baking sheet.

5. Bake pavlovas for 1 hour and 15 minutes. Turn oven off, open the door slightly, and let pavlovas rest in oven another 30 minutes.

6. Remove from oven and garnish with whipped cream, fresh fruits, honey or jam, mint, or whatever you wish.

Whipped Cream

Servings:16
Total Time: 10 minutes

This go-to homemade Whipped Cream recipe is easy to whip up anytime. Try different extract flavors to alter the taste slightly for all types of desserts!

INGREDIENTS

- 1 cup heavy cream
- 1 tablespoon confectioners' sugar
- 1 teaspoon vanilla extract

INSTRUCTIONS

1. Place beaters from hand mixer and a mixing bowl into the freezer to chill for 30 minutes.

2. Once cold, remove the beaters and mixing bowl from freezer and beat the heavy cream, confectioners' sugar, and vanilla extract for about 7 minutes until stiff peaks form. A stiff peak is achieved when the beaters are removed from whipped cream and the whipped cream does not flop over.

3. Serve.

Variations

Swap 1 teaspoon vanilla extract for extract of choice. Peppermint and hazelnut are especially delicious.

Nutter Butter Balls

Servings: 32
Total Time: 40 minutes

These are the easiest peanut butter balls you will ever make! Nutter butter cookies add the perfect amount of peanut butter flavoring and are mixed with cream cheese for creamy treats engulfed in chocolate and topped with a crunchy peanut garnish.

INGREDIENTS

1 (1 pound) package Nutter Butter cookies

8 ounces cream cheese

10 ounces milk chocolate melting wafers

Chopped peanuts, for garnish

INSTRUCTIONS

1. Place Nutter Butter cookies into food processor and pulse into crumbs.

2. Add in cream cheese and pulse again until fully mixed.

3. Use a cookie scoop to measure out each ball, then roll balls in the palms of your hands and place onto parchment paper. Let cool in fridge for 30 minutes.

4. Melt the chocolate wafers in a microwave-safe container or mug in 30 second increments, stirring between, until melted.

5. Dip each ball into melted chocolate and place back on parchment paper. I like to use a fork and a knife to assist me in dipping.

6. Immediately add chopped peanuts on top.

7. Repeat process for each ball.

8. Let set, then serve.

Acknowledgments

Writing a cookbook came with a lot of ups and downs and dirty dishes. A big thank you to my husband, Aaron, for coming home from work after a long day and helping to tackle the pile of dirty dishes taking over our kitchen. Trust me, there were some crazy days when creating this book! Also, thank you for putting so many weekend plans on hold so I could spend the day developing a recipe or shooting an image for this book.

My children are my everything so I cannot go without giving them a huge thank you. Our home was full of cookies, candies, chocolates, and other sweet treats for months! I am sure it was somewhat torture to have all these untouchable goodies laying around. You patiently waited while I worked on each recipe and board to be my taste testers and giving honest criticism on the look and taste of everything. At times, painfully honest, but it helped me tremendously with building a better book.

Thank you to the Skyhorse Publishing team. I never imagined that I would get the opportunity to write my own cookbook, but you gave me the motivation and guidance to press on and make it happen.

Special thank you to my parents. You always made food a way to connect and spend more quality time together, whether it be one of Dad's special breakfast omelets before school or a simple family weeknight dinner sitting around the table. Food has always been more than just eating out of necessity. Sharing a meal can gather people together and be a way to bond. Thank you for teaching me this growing up.

Thank you to my tiny sidekick, my cat, Chloe, who supervised the entire creation of this book. Every single recipe, every single photo, every single page was silently judged and criticized by her. I hope you don't totally hate the book, Chloe, and now you can return to your regularly scheduled nap routine since the book creation process is over. Oh, and you were correct about too many salted chocolate caramels being on that Chocolate Tasting Board. Thank you for removing some for me and throwing them off the counter.

A thank you to my late grandmother. Without her guidance, I am not sure I would have found the joy in cooking that I feel now.

I did not forget about you, too, Grandma Jones. You always know how to throw a wonderful party with beautifully presented foods and drinks. That eye for detail and meticulous planning also runs through my blood. So, thank you.

Conwversion Charts

METRIC AND IMPERIAL CONVERSIONS
(These conversions are rounded for convenience)

Ingredient	Cups/Tablespoons/ Teaspoons	Ounces	Grams/Milliliters
Butter	1 cup/ 16 tablespoons/ 2 sticks	8 ounces	230 grams
Cheese, shredded	1 cup	4 ounces	110 grams
Cream cheese	1 tablespoon	0.5 ounce	14.5 grams
Cornstarch	1 tablespoon	0.3 ounce	8 grams
Flour, all-purpose	1 cup/1 tablespoon	4.5 ounces/0.3 ounce	125 grams/8 grams
Flour, whole wheat	1 cup	4 ounces	120 grams
Fruit, dried	1 cup	4 ounces	120 grams
Fruits or veggies, chopped	1 cup	5 to 7 ounces	145 to 200 grams
Fruits or veggies, pureed	1 cup	8.5 ounces	245 grams
Honey, maple syrup, or corn syrup	1 tablespoon	0.75 ounce	20 grams
Liquids: cream, milk, water, or juice	1 cup	8 fluid ounces	240 milliliters
Oats	1 cup	5.5 ounces	150 grams
Salt	1 teaspoon	0.2 ounce	6 grams
Spices: cinnamon, cloves, ginger, or nutmeg (ground)	1 teaspoon	0.2 ounce	5 milliliters
Sugar, brown, firmly packed	1 cup	7 ounces	200 grams
Sugar, white	1 cup/1 tablespoon	7 ounces/0.5 ounce	200 grams/12.5 grams
Vanilla extract	1 teaspoon	0.2 ounce	4 grams

OVEN TEMPERATURES

Fahrenheit	Celsius	Gas Mark
225°	110°	¼
250°	120°	½
275°	140°	1
300°	150°	2
325°	160°	3
350°	180°	4
375°	190°	5
400°	200°	6
425°	220°	7
450°	230°	8

Index